ABT

U.S. WARS

THE KOREAN WAR

A MyReportLinks.com Book

Jeff C. Young

MyReportLinks.com Books

an imprint of

Enslow Publishers, Inc.

Box 398, 40 Industrial Road
Berkeley Heights, NJ 07922
USA

To my niece, Christina Marie Davila.

MyReportLinks.com Books, an imprint of Enslow Publishers, Inc. MyReportLinks is a trademark of Enslow Publishers, Inc.

Library of Congress Cataloging-in-Publication Data

Young, Jeff C., 1948–
  The Korean War / Jeff C. Young.
    p. cm. — (U.S. wars)
Summary: Presents the background to, and military and political aspects of, the Korean War. Includes internet links to web sites.
Includes bibliographical references and index.
  ISBN 0-7660-5148-X
  1. Korean War, 1950–1953—Juvenile literature. [1. Korean War, 1950–1953.] I. Title. II. Series.
  DS918 .Y675 2003
  951.904'2—dc21
              2002153589

Printed in the United States of America

10 9 8 7 6 5 4 3 2 1

To Our Readers:
Through the purchase of this book, you and your library gain access to the Report Links that specifically back up this book.
The Publisher will provide access to the Report Links that back up this book and will keep these Report Links up to date on **www.myreportlinks.com** for three years from the book's first publication date.
We have done our best to make sure all Internet addresses in this book were active and appropriate when we went to press. However, the author and the Publisher have no control over, and assume no liability for, the material available on those Internet sites or on other Web sites they may link to.
The usage of the MyReportLinks.com Books Web site is subject to the terms and conditions stated on the Usage Policy Statement on **www.myreportlinks.com**.
A password may be required to access the Report Links that back up this book. The password is found on the bottom of page 4 of this book.
Any comments or suggestions can be sent by e-mail to comments@myreportlinks.com or to the address on the back cover.

Photo Credits: American Battle Monuments Commission, p. 45; CNN.com/Cold War, pp. 30, 32; © Corel Corporation, p. 3; © 2001 War Eagles Air Museum; Dwight D. Eisenhower Library, p. 37; Enslow Publishers, Inc., pp. 11, 41; Library of Congress, pp. 15, 43; MyReportLinks.com Books, p. 4; National Archives, pp. 13, 20, 24, 25, 28, 34, 36, 39; Official Marine Corps Photograph, from the "All Hands" collection at the Naval Historical Center, pp. 19, 21; United States of America Korean War Commemoration, p. 23; U.S. Army Center of Military History, pp. 1, 26, 35.

Cover Photo: U.S. Army Center of Military History

Cover Description: *Breakthrough at Chipyong-ni*

Contents

MyReportLinks.com Books
Great Books, Great Links, Great for Research!

MyReportLinks.com Books present the information you need to learn about your report subject. In addition, they show you where to go on the Internet for more information. The pre-evaluated Report Links that back up this book are kept up to date on **www.myreportlinks.com**. With the purchase of a MyReportLinks.com Books title, you and your library gain access to the Report Links that specifically back up that book. The Report Links save hours of research time and link to dozens—even hundreds—of Web sites, source documents, and photos related to your report topic.

Please see "To Our Readers" on the Copyright page for important information about this book, the MyReportLinks.com Books Web site, and the Report Links that back up this book.

Access:

The Publisher will provide access to the Report Links that back up this book and will try to keep these Report Links up to date on our Web site for three years from the book's first publication date. Please enter **AKW3076** if asked for a password.

Report Links

The Internet sites described below can be accessed at
http://www.myreportlinks.com

*EDITOR'S CHOICE

▶ **Korean War: The Forgotten War**
Military.com provides a comprehensive discussion of the Korean War.
Here you will find an overview of different phases of the war, biographies
of key players, documents related to the war, maps, and a time line. You
can also read media depictions of events that occurred during the war.
Link to this Internet site from http://www.myreportlinks.com

*EDITOR'S CHOICE

▶ **United States of America Korean War Commemoration**
The Korean War Commemoration Web site is a repository of valuable
information on the Korean War. It provides a detailed chronology
augmented with maps, testimonials from veterans, biographies of key
figures, and photographs from battles.
Link to this Internet site from http://www.myreportlinks.com

*EDITOR'S CHOICE

▶ **Remembering the Korean War**
The United States Army Web site provides a detailed military history of
the Korean War. It contains the full text of several official accounts
published by the Center for Military History, each covering a different
aspect of Korean War.
Link to this Internet site from http://www.myreportlinks.com

*EDITOR'S CHOICE

▶ **MacArthur**
PBS's Web site provides and in-depth look at the life of General Douglas
MacArthur, who led the Korean War effort until being removed from his
command by President Truman. Truman's firing of MacArthur is only one
of the events discussed on this site.
Link to this Internet site from http://www.myreportlinks.com

*EDITOR'S CHOICE

▶ **Truman Presidential Museum and Library**
At the Truman Presidential Museum and Library Web site you can explore
the life and presidency of Harry S Truman, who was in office at the start
of the Korean War. The site contains a wealth of material on Truman's life
and contributions.
Link to this Internet site from http://www.myreportlinks.com

*EDITOR'S CHOICE

▶ **War Eagles Air Museum**
At the War Eagles Air Museum you take a virtual tour through the
museum's exhibits where you will learn about aircrafts, automobiles, and
military equipment used in World War II and the Korean War.

Link to this Internet site from http://www.myreportlinks.com

 The Internet sites described below can be accessed at
http://www.myreportlinks.com

▶ **Arlington National Cemetery: May 13, 1864**
America's Story from America's Library, a Library of Congress Web site, tells the
story of Arlington Cemetery in Virginia. Here you will learn about the first
soldier who was buried there and traditions that take place on Memorial Day at
the cemetery.

Link to this Internet site from http://www.myreportlinks.com

▶ **Blood, Sweat, and Saline: Combat Medicine in the Korean Conflict**
This exhibit from the National Museum of Health & Medicine explores
what it was like to treat the soldiers who fought in the Korean War.

Link to this Internet site from http://www.myreportlinks.com

▶ **CNN Cold War Series: Episode 5-Korea**
Explore the Korean War through the CNN Interactive Cold War series.
Here you will find interactive maps, historical documents, and articles
related to the Korean War.

Link to this Internet site from http://www.myreportlinks.com

▶ **The Cold War Museum**
The Cold War Museum Web site offers a comprehensive history of the Cold
War. There is a time line that guides you through the six decades of the Cold
War, an image gallery, and much more. Click on the "50s" to read about the
Korean War.

Link to this Internet site from http://www.myreportlinks.com

▶ *Combat Support in Korea*
Combat Support in Korea is a collection of interviews with military persons
who served in the Korean War. Broken up into nine chapters, there are over one
hundred firsthand accounts of experiences had by those who served
in the war.

Link to this Internet site from http://www.myreportlinks.com

▶ **CyberSchool Bus**
CyberSchool Bus is a United Nations Web site designed specifically for kids.
Here you can explore and learn about the member countries of the United
Nations. You can also explore the history of the United Nations.

Link to this Internet site from http://www.myreportlinks.com

Report Links

The Internet sites described below can be accessed at
http://www.myreportlinks.com

▶ **Dwight Eisenhower: The Cautious Warrior**
This Web site provides a comprehensive biography of Dwight Eisenhower.
Here you will learn about his life before, during, and after his presidency.
You will also learn how Eisenhower negotiated a cease-fire in the Korean
War, which resulted in Korea being divided at the 38th parallel.

Link to this Internet site from http://www.myreportlinks.com

▶ **Fast Attacks & Boomers**
Fast Attacks & Boomers, a Smithsonian Institute Web site, provides
a brief look at the Korean War. You will also learn about the Cold War,
submarines, and nuclear weapons.

Link to this Internet site from http://www.myreportlinks.com

▶ **History of the World Timeline: Korean War**
The History Channel's History of The World Timeline offers a unique
chance to see the Korean War alongside other important events during
this time period. You will also find links for further reading.

Link to this Internet site from http://www.myreportlinks.com

▶ **Korea + 50: No Longer Forgotten**
This site is produced by the official libraries of Harry S Truman and
Dwight Eisenhower. It draws on the extensive collection of primary
sources and firsthand accounts from both libraries. The Web site is
enhanced by a collection of black and white and full color photos.

Link to this Internet site from http://www.myreportlinks.com

▶ **Korea & *M*A*S*H*: A War Remembered**
The *M*A*S*H* series was a television show which first aired in 1972.
The show was based on those who worked at Mobile Army Surgical
Hospital during the Korean War. At this Web site you can view an exhibit
dedicated to the program.

Link to this Internet site from http://www.myreportlinks.com

▶ **Korea: Recollections of the Korean War, 1950–1953**
The Korea: Recollections of the Korean War, 1950–1953 Web site holds
the text of recollections from those who fought in the Korean War.

Link to this Internet site from http://www.myreportlinks.com

 The Internet sites described below can be accessed at
http://www.myreportlinks.com

▶**The Korean War**
"The Korean War" provides detailed chronological information of the Korean War—the air war in particular. Among its content is a graphical list of countries that participated in the war with detailed information on the role that each country played.

Link to this Internet site from http://www.myreportlinks.com

▶**The Korean War, June 1950–July 1953**
From the Department of the Navy—Naval Historical Center, comes this Web site which provides a pictorial and historical overview of events that occurred during the Korean War.

Link to this Internet site from http://www.myreportlinks.com

▶**Korean War.net**
The Korean War.net Web site's strength lies in its large collection of articles on various topics relevant to the Korean War. The articles cover not only historical topics but also current issues rooted in the outcome of the Korean War. The site also contains scans of original documents.

Link to this Internet site from http://www.myreportlinks.com

▶**The Korean War: An Overview**
Part of the BBC's *Wars and Conflict* series, this site traces the major events of the Korean War in the context of the mounting Cold War between the Western democracies and the Eastern Block Communist nations. It is organized into four main periods of the war, and provides links for further reading.

Link to this Internet site from http://www.myreportlinks.com

▶**The Korean War Project**
The Korean War Project Web site is a memorial dedicated to those lost or missing in the Korean War. It also serves as a comprehensive resource center for information on the war. It includes an extensive list of scanned military maps, links to detailed historical information, and firsthand accounts.

Link to this Internet site from http://www.myreportlinks.com

▶**Korean War Veteran Memorial**
At the National Park Service Web site you can visit the Korean War Veterans Memorial located in Washington D.C. Click on "InDepth" to learn more about the memorial and its history.

Link to this Internet site from http://www.myreportlinks.com

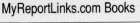
Report Links

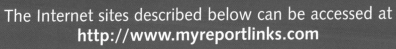

The Internet sites described below can be accessed at
http://www.myreportlinks.com

▶ NSA Korean War 1950–1953 Commemoration
The National Security Association Web site provides pictures of Korean flags, maps, and papers written about the Korean War.

Link to this Internet site from http://www.myreportlinks.com

▶ People & Events: The Korean War
PBS' Race for the Superbomb Web site provides a brief overview of the Korean War as it pertained to nuclear weapons.

Link to this Internet site from http://www.myreportlinks.com

▶ The United Nations Security Council
The United Nations Security Council was called upon to address North Korea's invasion of South Korea in 1950. The UN played a large role in the Korean War.

Link to this Internet site from http://www.myreportlinks.com

▶ The United States Enters the Korean Conflict
The National Archives Web site provides a brief overview of the Korean conflict and links to President Truman's document stating his decision to send air and naval forces to assist in defending South Korea.

Link to this Internet site from http://www.myreportlinks.com

▶ Veterans Day November 11
America's Story from America's Library, a Library of Congress Web site, tells the story of Veterans Day. Learn why Veterans Day was initially called Armistice Day, and about the many different ways people celebrate this day.

Link to this Internet site from http://www.myreportlinks.com

▶ War Powers Resolution: Presidential Compliance
The United States went to war in Korea without a formal declaration of war by Congress. Since then, legislation has been passed in Congress which requires that no troops may be sent overseas for more than sixty days without approval from Congress.

Link to this Internet site from http://www.myreportlinks.com

▶ Combatants

South Korea and the *United States:* Aided by members of the United Nations Command, which included Australia; Belgium; Canada; Colombia; Ethiopia; France; Great Britain; Luxembourg; the Netherlands; New Zealand; the Philippines; South Africa; Thailand; and Turkey.

North Korea: Alongside China with some support from the Soviet Union.

CASUALTIES[1]	KILLED	WOUNDED	POW/MIA
United States	36,516	103,284	5,178
South Korea	58,127	175,743	166,297
UN Command	3,194	11,297	2,769
North Korea	522,000 dead or wounded and 102,000 POWs.		
China	945,000 dead or wounded and 22,000 POWs.		

*An estimated 1 million South Korean civilians were killed. There are no reliable estimates for North Korean civilians.

▶ A Brief Time Line

1950 —*June 25:* North Korea invades South Korea.

—*July 5:* U.S. troops and North Korean troops fight for the first time at the Battle of Osan.

—*Aug. 1:* Retreating U.S. and South Korean troops form the Pusan Perimeter.

—*Sept. 15:* U.S. and United Nations Command (UNC) troops launch an invasion at Inchon, South Korea.

—*Oct. 1:* U.S. troops cross the 38th parallel and enter North Korea.

—*Oct. 14:* Chinese troops enter North Korea.

—*Oct. 19:* UNC forces capture the North Korean capital of Pyongyang.

—*Dec.:* UNC forces are driven back. Communist forces launch a major offensive and recross the 38th parallel into South Korea.

1951 —*Jan. 5:* South Korean capital of Seoul is recaptured by Communist forces.

—*March 18:* Seoul is retaken by the UNC forces.

—*April 11:* General Douglas MacArthur is relieved of the command of U.S. and UNC forces by President Harry S Truman.

—*July 10:* Peace talks begin.

1952 —*May 7:* Both sides announce a stalemate in peace talks over the POW issue.

1953 —March 30: China agrees to an exchange of sick and wounded POWs.

—*May 28:* U.S. and United Nations negotiating team presents their final terms for peace.

—*July 27:* Armistice (truce) ending the fighting is signed at Panmunjom.

Predawn Attack

Since the end of World War II in 1945, there had been on-again, off-again fighting along the 38th parallel dividing North and South Korea. There had been rumors that Communist North Korea was going to invade South Korea. One report in March 1950 predicted the invasion would occur three months later.

▶ Shaken Silence

Still, the predawn attack on June 25, 1950 took both South Korea and the United States by surprise. Around 4:00 A.M., the stillness along the border was shattered by the sounds of exploding mortar shells. The slumbering South Korean Army was woefully unprepared for the massive invasion that followed.

About an hour after the first shells began exploding,

The Korean War began on ▶ June 25, 1959, when North Korea attacked South Korea and crossed the 38th parallel.

North Korean tanks were spotted on roads leading to the South Korean border. Behind the tanks were thousands of well armed and well trained North Korean soldiers.

The defending South Korean army was poorly prepared and badly outnumbered. The North Korean army consisted of 135,000 highly motivated, combat-ready soldiers. The South Korean army only had about 95,000 men. Only about one third of that army was deployed along the 38th parallel when the North Koreans attacked.

The opening barrage of artillery and mortar fire allowed the North Korean tanks and troops to quickly advance southward. During the first days of the invasion, the North Korean army advanced nonstop. Occasionally, the South Korean army would put up some resistance, but North Korean tanks sent the South Koreans retreating. The South Koreans had no tanks or antitank weapons of their own to stop the advance.

▶ News Reaches the United States

News of the attack reached Washington, D.C., on Saturday night, June 24. President Harry S Truman abruptly ended his vacation in Independence, Missouri, to return to Washington. He quickly convened meetings with officials from the State Department and the Department of Defense. They discussed plans for a United States response to the invasion. The United States at this time had a policy of trying to stop the spread of communist governments such as North Korea's.

During Truman's absence from Washington, U.S. Secretary of State Dean Acheson took charge. Acheson called the Secretary General of the United Nations and asked him to convene a meeting of the United Nations (UN) Security Council. On Sunday, June 25, the Security

Council held an emergency meeting. It passed a resolution calling for an immediate end to the hostilities. The resolution also called for North Korea to withdraw its forces from South Korea. However, any hopes of a quick end to the conflict were shattered when the North Korean government ignored the United Nations resolution.

America Enters the War

While flying back to Washington, President Truman thought about how World War II had begun and how the Korean conflict could set off a third world war. He would later write:

> I remembered how each time that the democracies failed to act it encouraged the aggressors to keep going ahead. . . . If the Communists were permitted to force their way into the Republic of Korea without opposition from the free world, no small nation would have the courage to resist threats and aggression by stronger Communist neighbors. If this was allowed to go it would mean a third world war, just as similar incidents had brought on the second world war.[1]

▶ *Worried that the crisis in Korea might cause World War III, President Harry S Truman authorized the bombing of North Korea and sent American ground troops the area on June 29, 1950.*

Truman and his advisors agreed that the North Koreans had to be stopped, but they disagreed on how. Some military advisors argued for a combination of naval forces and air power to drive them out of South Korea. Other advisors argued that ground forces would also have to be deployed.

As North Korean troops advanced on the South Korean capital of Seoul, the United States and the UN showed their resolve to halt the attack. On June 27, Truman authorized the United States air and naval forces south of the 38th parallel to aid the South Koreans. That same day, the UN Security Council asked its member nations to aid South Korea in repelling the attack.

On June 28, the North Koreans captured Seoul. The next day, Truman authorized the bombing of North Korea and sending American ground troops to Korea. On July 1, the first American troops arrived in Korea. The troops were sent thousands of miles from home to fight a war that would officially be called a "police action."

Korea From 1910 to 1945

Since 1910, Korea had been a Japanese colony. Japan's domination of Korea ended when Japan was defeated by the United States and its allies in World War II.

After World War II ended in 1945, Korea was divided into two areas. The United States and the Soviet Union agreed that the 38th parallel would be the border between North and South Korea. The 38th parallel is an imaginary line that follows 38 degrees longitude on a map. The Soviets would occupy and control North Korea. American

▲ In June 1950, General Douglas MacArthur (left) met with South Korea's President Syngman Rhee (right) at Suwon airstrip, twenty miles south of Seoul.

troops would remain in South Korea while the United States oversaw the new nation.

In September 1947, the United States tried to reunite Korea by asking the UN General Assembly to supervise a nationwide election. The UN agreed, and asked that all foreign troops be withdrawn from Korea after a new government was elected and took power. However, North Korea refused to participate.

▶ An Attempt at Democracy

In South Korea, the American-backed candidate, Syngman Rhee, was elected the first president of the Republic of Korea (ROK). Rhee had once been imprisoned and tortured by the Japanese for advocating Korean independence. Rhee was an anti-Communist who wanted to topple the government of North Korea.

The Soviet Union prevented free elections in North Korea. The Soviets refused to allow UN observers entry into North Korea. Kim Il Sung was named as the premier of the newly formed Democratic People's Republic of Korea (DPRK). Kim also had fought for Korean independence from Japan. In World War II, he had served in the Soviet Army. By the end of 1948, the Soviets had withdrawn their troops from North Korea.

The last American troops were removed from South Korea at the end of June 1949.

About five hundred United States officers and soldiers were left behind to serve as an "advisory group."

▶ Political Tug-O-War

The formation of two opposing Korean governments added to an already tense situation. Each government claimed they were the only legitimate ruler of Korea. Both

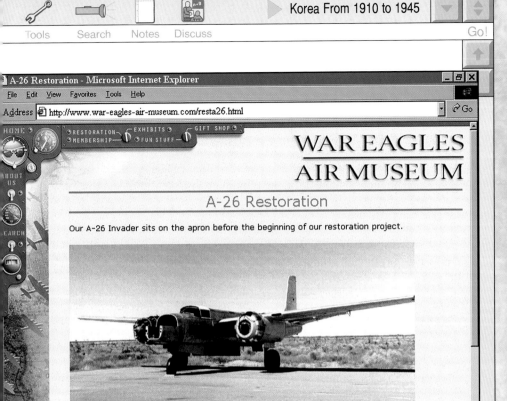

WAR EAGLES
AIR MUSEUM

A-26 Restoration

Our A-26 Invader sits on the apron before the beginning of our restoration project.

Internet

▲ *The A-26 "Invader" was used in tactical intruder missions during the Korean War. The War Eagles Air Museum restores historical aircraft such as the A-26 shown here.*

countries maintained a standing army and stifled political dissent. There were sporadic border skirmishes between the two Koreas.

Although he was democratically elected, Rhee became a ruthless dictator. He took steps to bring the police under his personal control. Rhee's main political rival, Kim Ku, was assassinated in his own home. Concern over Rhee's behavior caused the United States to deny Rhee's request to give his army armor and heavy artillery.

The United States had two reasons for withholding tanks, artillery, and aircraft from the South Koreans. The

first reason was that most of the military equipment that the United States exported went to Greece and Turkey to halt the advance of Communism in Eastern Europe. Also, the United States was cautious because of Rhee's remarks toward North Korea. Rhee openly boasted that if he had sufficient weapons (planes and tanks), he would invade North Korea and overthrow Kim Il Sung's government.

Rhee's threats made the United States cautious and uneasy. The prevailing opinion in Washington was that an invasion of North Korea by South Korea would set off World War III. There was a widely held belief that the Soviet Union and Communist China (People's Republic of China) would send ground troops and military assistance to help North Korea.

▶ "We Are Not at War"

After the fall of Seoul in June 1950, U.S. General Douglas MacArthur flew to Korea from Tokyo, Japan, for an eye-witness look at the fighting. MacArthur was appalled by what he saw. The ROK (South Korean) troops were under equipped, badly outnumbered, and hastily retreating. MacArthur advised Department of Defense officials and President Truman that United States ground troops were needed to halt the advance of the North Korean troops.

"The only hope of holding the present line (then just south of Seoul) is through the introduction of U.S. ground combat forces into the Korean battle area," MacArthur reported.[1]

On June 30, Truman approved a request for United States ground troops. He did so without seeking approval from Congress. He justified his action by saying he was worried that Congressional debate would delay the

▲ *U.S. Marines en route to the war front share candy with a couple of South Korean children.*

shipment of troops and arms. By then, it might be too late to save South Korea.

During his first press conference since the invasion, Truman asserted, "We are not at war."[2] Then a reporter asked: "Would it be correct to call this a police action under the United Nations?"[3] "Yes, Truman replied, "That is exactly what it amounts to."[4]

However, the so-called police action became a war even though war was not declared by the United States. There would be fierce, bloody fighting, resulting in millions of military and civilian casualties.

Early Problems Are Overcome

The first battle engaging United States troops found the Americans ill-equipped and woefully unprepared for combat. The confident United States troops expected the North Korean soldiers to lose their will to win when they realized that they were fighting Americans.

On July 5, 1950, the American army division known as the Eighth U.S. Army, Korea (EUSAK) attempted to stop the advancing North Korean People's Army (NKPA)

▲ UN forces were forced to retreat back across the 38th parallel in July 1950.

at the Battle of Osan. The fighting began at around 8:00 A.M. By 2:30 P.M., the EUSAK troops were retreating.

The NKPA troops easily moved southward behind the protective cover of Soviet-built tanks. The poorly equipped EUSAK units had no tanks of their own. They also lacked weapons that could break through armor—such as bazookas and antitank mines. The Americans were additionally hampered by old equipment and weapons. Most of their radios did not work, and their mortars and M-1 rifles were not suitable for combat.

Lieutenant Colonel Charles Smith ordered the EUSAK troops to retreat. It was a difficult and disheartening decision, but militarily it was the right decision. The NKPA enjoyed an overwhelming superiority in numbers and weapons.

Smith explained his decision to retreat by saying: "To stand and die or to try to get the remains of my Task Force out of there? I could last at best only another hour and then lose everything I had. I chose to try to get out, in hopes that we would live to fight another day."[1]

The soldiers who made up the EUSAK

Two Marines keep watch over ▷ the Pusan Perimeter by the Naktong River in August 1950.

units were not battle hardened and combat ready. They came to Korea after being stationed in Japan, where they had enjoyed a fairly safe assignment in a postwar, American-occupied country. Only a few EUSAK officers were combat veterans of World War II.

▷ Defeat at Osan

The first battle of the Korean War was a stunning defeat for the United States. About 150 of the 540 EUSAK soldiers in the Battle of Osan were killed, wounded, or missing in action. NKPA casualties were estimated at 42 dead and 85 wounded. The EUSAK's resistance held up the NKPA's southern advance for about seven hours.

The Battle of Osan was a shocking preview of things to come. Americans who had hoped for a quick and easy victory found the NKPA rapidly moving through South Korea in July and August 1950.

▷ Defensive Plan

In late July 1950, the EUSAK commander, Lieutenant General Walton Walker, met with MacArthur in Korea. They decided that their only hope of stopping the North Koreans was to retreat southward and then establish a defensive position. They decided to draw and defend a line north of the major port city of Pusan along the Naktong River.

On July 29, Walker met with the officers responsible for organizing the defensive perimeter (line to be defended). He told them that if the line did not hold then the war was practically over.

"We are fighting a battle against time," Walker said. "There will be no more retreating. . . . There is no line behind us to which we can retreat. . . . We must fight until

Tools   Search   Notes   Discuss   Go!

IMAGES

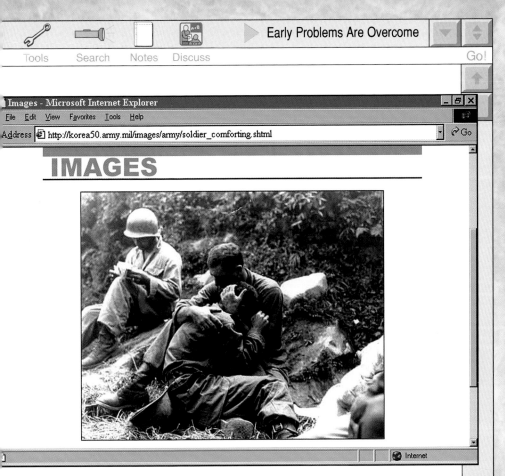

Images - Microsoft Internet Explorer

File   Edit   View   Favorites   Tools   Help

Address http://korea50.army.mil/images/army/soldier_comforting.shtml   Go

Internet

▲ *An American infantryman is comforted by another soldier, in August 1950, after learning that a friend was killed in action. Over thirty-six thousand American soldiers died in the Korean War.*

the end. We will fight as a team. If some of us die, we will die fighting together."[2]

EUSAK soldiers were given a "stand or die" order. With the sea at their backs, retreating was no longer an option. There was no place else to go.

On August 1, EUSAK and ROK troops began establishing their defensive position along the Naktong River. The line of troops stretched 150 miles, across the entire country. While they were preparing to defend their position, attacks by the United Nations Command (UNC) units under MacArthur's command were weakening the

▲ *In an attempt to cut North Korea's communications, the USS Missouri was ordered to bombard Chong Jin, Korea.*

advancing NKPA. UNC units were the name given to the combined Allied forces.

American, Australian, and British planes were bombing NKPA troops and supply convoys. North Korean soldiers advancing down the east coast of Korea were being bombarded by offshore warships. The oppressive summer heat and seasonal monsoons (rainstorms) were also sapping the strength of the North Korean soldiers.

Under MacArthur's leadership, the UNC units were coming together as a fighting force. A total of fifteen UN member nations sent soldiers, arms, and planes to fight the NKPA.

Tools   Search   Notes   Discuss   Go!

The Pusan Perimeter

In spite of the weather and the various counteroffensives, the NKPA troops pressed on toward Pusan. The infusion of additional EUSAK and UNC forces allowed the defenders to establish a defensive line known as the Pusan Perimeter. The arc-shaped line stretched about one hundred miles from north to south and around fifty miles from east to west.

The six-week series of engagements that became known as the Battle of the Pusan Perimeter began on the evening of July 31, 1950. Several times, the NKPA troops

Members of the Marine Corps are often referred to as leathernecks. On September 15, 1950, these leathernecks used scaling ladders in an amphibious invasion of Inchon.

http://www.army.mil/cmh-pg/photos/Korea/kor1950/SC351390.jpg - Microsoft Internet Explorer

File   Edit   View   Favorites   Tools   Help

Address   http://www.army.mil/cmh-pg/photos/Korea/kor1950/SC351390.jpg   Go

351/390

Done   Internet

▲ *A member of UN forces fires into a street in Seoul, South Korea.*

broke through the line, but they were always repelled by Walker and MacArthur's superior firepower. In late August, the NKPA launched an all-out attack on Pusan. They got to within fifty miles of the vital port city.

The setbacks sustained by the NKPA secured Pusan and left the North Koreans vulnerable to a major counterattack. MacArthur came up with a daring and dangerous plan to expand the Korean conflict into a two-front war. This meant that the UN and United States forces would be fighting in two separate areas at the same time. He selected the port city of Inchon for a counterattack.

▶ Inchon

Inchon was Korea's second largest port and was located only fifteen miles from Seoul. The area in and around Inchon was important for transporting NKPA supplies. Capturing the area would cut off vital supply lines to NKPA troops attacking the Pusan Perimeter. Also, capturing Seoul from the North Koreans would be a serious blow to the morale of the NKPA.

High-ranking United States military officials strongly objected to MacArthur's plan. Warships would have to navigate a narrow and shallow channel to reach Inchon. Military intelligence did not know if the harbor was filled with land mines. They argued that too many things could go wrong.

MacArthur overcame their objections by claiming: "By seizing Seoul (after taking Inchon) I would completely paralyze the enemy's supply system. Without munitions and food they will soon be helpless and disorganized, and can easily be overpowered."[3]

MacArthur's arguments convinced President Truman to approve of the Inchon strategy. On September 15, 1950, a force of 262 ships and 70,000 soldiers attacked Inchon. The NKPA was taken by surprise. It took less than a day for MacArthur's forces to capture Inchon. Eleven days after the invasion, Seoul was recaptured. At the same time, General Walker's EUSAK forces began moving north. The NKPA found itself trapped between two advancing armies.

Now the North Koreans were the ones on the run and retreating. There was a renewed sense of optimism that the war would soon be over.

Chapter 4

Back-and-Forth

With the NKPA retreating north of the 38th parallel, the United States and the UN were confronted with a very difficult decision. It was whether to keep the pressure on the North Koreans by crossing the 38th parallel?

Under the terms of the UN resolution their mission was ". . . to repel the armed attack and restore international peace and security in the area."[1] However, with the NKPA in retreat, there was an opportunity to conquer North Korea and reunite the country.

▲ American forces examine the North Korean position on the war front.

▷ The 38th Parallel

The major concern was that crossing the 38th parallel could cause China or the Soviet Union to enter the war. President Truman, the Joint Chiefs of Staff (the chief of staffs of the U.S. Army, Air Force and Navy), and most Congressional leaders favored the invasion of North Korea. They believed that the objective of fighting a war was total victory. If we did not pursue them, the NKPA would regroup, rearm, and then launch a later attack.

Truman did not think there was much chance of China or the Soviet Union entering the war. According to United States intelligence reports, China did not want to get involved in the Korean War. The Soviets had done nothing to stop intervention by the UN. Their apparent attitude was one of indifference.

In late September, MacArthur received permission from Truman and the Joint Chiefs of Staff (JCS) to cross into North Korea. His primary mission was to destroy the NKPA. His secondary mission was to reunite the country under the leadership of Syngman Rhee. If China or the Soviet Union showed any interest in joining the war, he would have to immediately notify Washington.

Truman and the JCS placed a couple of additional stipulations upon MacArthur. He could not send any aircraft across the Chinese border. Additionally, no non-Korean ground troops could be used in the North Korean provinces that bordered China and the Soviet Union. MacArthur responded to those orders by declaring: "I regard all of Korea open for our military operations."[2]

For some reason MacArthur was not asked to clarify that statement. His stubborn refusal to obey directives and orders would eventually lead to his dismissal.

Back   Forward   Stop   Review   Home   Explore   Favorites   History

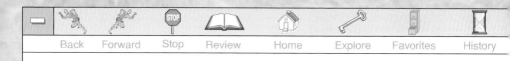

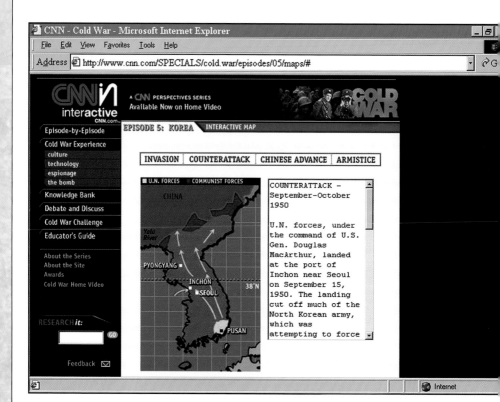

CNN - Cold War - Microsoft Internet Explorer

File   Edit   View   Favorites   Tools   Help

Address http://www.cnn.com/SPECIALS/cold.war/episodes/05/maps/#

interactive
CNN.com

A CNN PERSPECTIVES SERIES
Available Now on Home Video

COLD WAR

Episode-by-Episode

Cold War Experience
  culture
  technology
  espionage
  the bomb
Knowledge Bank
Debate and Discuss
Cold War Challenge
Educator's Guide

About the Series
About the Site
Awards
Cold War Home Video

RESEARCH *it:*

Feedback

EPISODE 5: KOREA   INTERACTIVE MAP

INVASION | COUNTERATTACK | CHINESE ADVANCE | ARMISTICE

U.N. FORCES   COMMUNIST FORCES

CHINA

Yalu River

PYONGYANG

INCHON
SEOUL
38'N

PUSAN

COUNTERATTACK –
September–October
1950

U.N. forces, under
the command of U.S.
Gen. Douglas
MacArthur, landed
at the port of
Inchon near Seoul
on September 15,
1950. The landing
cut off much of the
North Korean army,
which was
attempting to force

Internet

On September 15, 1950, General MacArthur launched the UN's counterattack by landing at the port of Inchon. UN troops pushing southward recaptured Seoul eleven days later. On October 19, UN troops took control of North Korea's capital, Pyongyang.

The first UNC troops crossed the 38th parallel on October 1. Eight days later a full scale invasion was underway. By October 19, the UNC forces had captured the North Korean capital of Pyongyang.

Chinese Involvement

While North Korea was being attacked, the Chinese nervously watched the UNC troops move closer to their border. On October 3, Chinese premier Chou En-lai issued a warning that China would come to the aid of NKPA if

UNC troops crossed the 38th parallel. United States Secretary of State Dean Acheson and military intelligence still believed that the Chinese were bluffing. They thought Chou's statement was a ploy to stop the invasion of North Korea.

MacArthur was also confident that the Chinese would not intervene. In mid-October he met with Truman and reassured the president that the Chinese would stay out of the Korean War. He told Truman that the EUSAK troops would be out of Korea and back in Japan by Christmas. When Truman and MacArthur ended their meeting, they both believed the war would soon be over.

While Truman and MacArthur were meeting, Chinese troops were secretly moving toward the North Korean border. They traveled on foot, so enemy planes could not detect any convoys of jeeps and trucks. The Chinese only traveled at night and wore civilian clothing over their uniforms. They did not even light fires for cooking, which would have set off clouds of smoke and gave away their position.

Skirmish

As the UNC troops advanced north from Pyongyang, the Chinese stealthily moved south. On October 25, the two armies met and fought for the first time. Their first skirmish occurred about fifty miles south of the Chinese border. A ROK battalion of about 750 soldiers was forced to turn back. About half of the battalion was either killed, wounded, or captured.

The ROK battalion did capture two enemy soldiers. When the enemy POWs were questioned, the South Koreans were astonished to find that they were Chinese. Initially, MacArthur denied that China had entered the

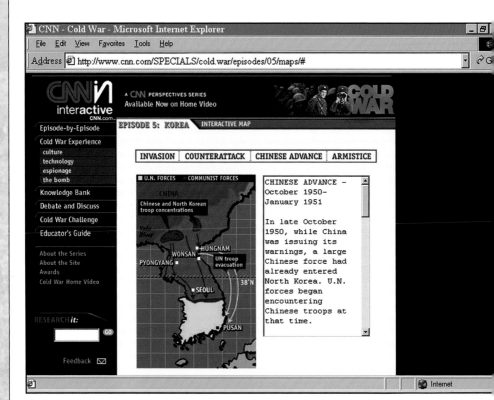

CNN - Cold War - Microsoft Internet Explorer

File Edit View Favorites Tools Help

Address http://www.cnn.com/SPECIALS/cold.war/episodes/05/maps/#

A CNN PERSPECTIVES SERIES
Available Now on Home Video

interactive
CNN.com

Episode-by-Episode

Cold War Experience
  culture
  technology
  espionage
  the bomb
Knowledge Bank
Debate and Discuss
Cold War Challenge
Educator's Guide

About the Series
About the Site
Awards
Cold War Home Video

RESEARCH it:

Feedback

EPISODE 5: KOREA   INTERACTIVE MAP

INVASION | COUNTERATTACK | CHINESE ADVANCE | ARMISTICE

U.N. FORCES   COMMUNIST FORCES

CHINA

Chinese and North Korean
troop concentrations

Yalu
River

HUNGNAM
WONSAN
PYONGYANG

UN troop
evacuation

SEOUL

38'N

PUSAN

CHINESE ADVANCE –
October 1950–
January 1951

In late October
1950, while China
was issuing its
warnings, a large
Chinese force had
already entered
North Korea. U.N.
forces began
encountering
Chinese troops at
that time.

Internet

After taking control of the North Korean capital on October 19, UN troops were attacked by Chinese and North Korean forces on November 24. They recaptured Seoul, pushing the UN troops 30 miles south of the South Korean capital.

war. By November, he belatedly acknowledged that United States military intelligence had been wrong about China's intentions.

China would continue to surprise MacArthur. After pushing back UNC troops, the Chinese abruptly quit fighting. By November 6, they had disappeared. UNC planes and ground patrols vainly searched for them. Apparently, they either retreated back into China or went into hiding in the forests of North Korea.

Why they retreated is still a mystery. One theory is that they quit so the UN would debate and then halt

MacArthur's plan to push farther into North Korea. The Chinese hoped that their intervention would convince the UN to call off the invasion.

The Chinese have claimed their reason for withdrawing was ". . . to encourage the enemy's arrogance."[3]

MacArthur interpreted China's sudden disappearance as a virtual surrender. He made plans for another invasion of North Korea. He announced an objective of ending the war by Christmas.

A Plan Foiled

MacArthur's invasion plan split his army in two. One part of the army would move up the eastern part of North Korea. A second unit known as the X Corps would advance up the western area.

After seeing MacArthur's invasion, the Chinese decided to reenter North Korea. The Chinese easily got into the area between the locations of the United States and UN armies. The Chinese had a force of 180,000 to battle the eastern unit and another 120,000 to fight the X Corps. MacArthur's invasion force numbered 247,000.

On the night of November 25, the Chinese attacked MacArthur's outnumbered and divided army. Despite suffering heavy casualties from American defensive fire, the Chinese pushed the invaders back below the 38th parallel. Their attack resulted in the largest retreat in United States military history.

Seoul was recaptured by the NKPA on January 5, 1951. After retreating and regrouping, the UNC forces dug in 25 miles south of Seoul and then launched a counteroffensive. Led by General Matthew B. Ridgway, who was now in charge of the Eighth Army, the Allies recaptured Seoul on March 14, 1951. Once again, they crossed

▲ *Like many others, the Korean War left these two siblings homeless.
They searched through rubble for morsels of food and tried to keep
warm beside a small fire.*

the 38th parallel and put the Chinese and North Koreans
on the run. The military successes gave MacArthur
renewed vigor and ultimately put him on a collision
course with Truman.

▷ MacArthur Clashes With President Truman

Back in October 1950, MacArthur had exceeded his
authority by demanding North Korea's surrender. It is
believed that Truman did not question MacArthur at the
time because China had not yet entered the war.

Then on March 24, 1951, MacArthur went even further in defying and undermining his commander in chief.
Truman was preparing to make an announcement on pos-
sible peace negotiations. MacArthur had been advised that
the announcement was forthcoming. Still, MacArthur

issued a statement predicting a victory for the UNC forces and demanding that China surrender.

MacArthur's behavior was causing America's war allies to question who was really in charge. On April 11, 1951, Truman relieved MacArthur of his command because he felt MacArthur was ignoring his orders. Truman replaced MacArthur with General Ridgway.

MacArthur's dismissal is regarded as Truman's most unpopular presidential decision. MacArthur returned to the United States and received a hero's welcome while members of Congress called for Truman's impeachment. The Senate held hearings to investigate MacArthur's firing and Truman's conduct of the war. Eventually, though, most Americans came to accept Truman's decision.

American members of United Nations forces protect the 38th parallel.

End of the Fighting

President Truman's hopes for truce talks were realized after representatives of the United Nations Command and the Communist forces agreed to meet. Allied forces had held firm at the 38th parallel. Because their position was stable, peace talks could begin. The truce talks began on July 10, 1951. By late November it looked like a settlement was near. Both sides agreed to a cease-fire line, a supervisory commission to enforce the truce and a process for making the truce a permanent agreement.

However they could not reach an agreement on how to return the POWs. There were thousands of North Korean

▲ *Peace negotiations were held at Panmunjom, Korea.*

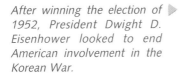

After winning the election of
1952, President Dwight D. Eisenhower looked to end American involvement in the Korean War.

and Chinese POWs who did not want to return to their homes because they feared the North Korean government. Plus, people in the South generally made a better living than in the North. The talks were also hampered by mutual stubbornness and distrust. Frequently, one of the two parties would boycott the talks.

On October 8, 1952, the UNC withdrew from the talks. They said that talks would resume only if the Communists would agree to a settlement of the POW repatriation issue. The failure to reach a settlement would cause the war to drag on for nine and a half more months.

The Election of General Eisenhower

As American casualties continued to rise, the war became a major issue in the 1952 presidential election. Truman had declined to seek reelection. The Democratic nominee was Governor Adlai Stevenson of Illinois. The Republican candidate was General Dwight D. Eisenhower.

Eisenhower's success in liberating Europe from the Nazis in World War II convinced many voters that he was the best candidate for ending the war. As a presidential candidate, he took full advantage of the war issue. In a

nationally televised speech on October 24, 1952, Eisenhower called Korea ". . . the burial ground of twenty-thousand American dead."[1]

Then, Eisenhower declared, "That job (ending the war) requires a personal trip to Korea. I shall make that trip. Only in that way could I learn best how to serve the American people in the course of peace. I shall go to Korea."[2]

After winning a landslide victory, Eisenhower visited Korea for three days in early December. He met with United States military leaders and South Korean President Syngman Rhee. He held a press conference before returning to the United States. Eisenhower made a statement indicating he wanted to end the war with a negotiated settlement. He said it was unlikely to achieve ". . . a positive and definite victory without possibly running the grave risk of enlarging the war."[3]

The Push For a Truce

Eisenhower's election helped to hasten the end of the war. Ending the war was a top priority and a campaign promise he intended to keep. Eisenhower's military background made the Chinese fearful that he may use nuclear weapons to end the Korean War. Thus, the Chinese were ready to negotiate a truce.

The push for a truce was also aided by the death of Soviet leader Joseph Stalin on March 5, 1953. A few days after Stalin's death, his successor, Georgi Malenkov, said that the Soviets believed they could settle disputes with any nation, including the United States, by negotiation.

Although the Soviet Union was not officially involved in the Korean War, it had a powerful influence over North Korea and China. The Soviets had sent advisors to help the

Chinese and North Koreans, and flew combat missions against United States' planes. Malenkov's willingness to mediate disputes influenced North Korea and China to compromise on the POW issue.

Operation Little Switch

In late March, North Korean and Chinese officials agreed to exchange sick and wounded POWs. On April 26, 1953, the first exchange of POWs occurred. One hundred and forty-nine Americans, 64 UNC soldiers, and 471 ROK soldiers were exchanged for 5,194 North Koreans, 1,034 Chinese, and 445 civilian POWs. The exchange was called Operation Little Switch.

Even though POWs were exchanged, heavy fighting was still going on. During the spring and summer of

▲ *United States Marines guard three North Korean POWs. The exchange of POWs was a major issue during peace talks between North and South Korea.*

1953, there were a number of small, seesaw battles around the western area of the 38th parallel. The best known of these was the Battle of Pork Chop Hill, which went on from March to July 1953. Pork Chop Hill came to symbolize the futile back-and-forth fighting of the war. After U.S. Marines fought valiantly to take and maintain Pork Chop Hill, they were evacuated. The slight tactical advantage of keeping the hill was not worth additional killed or wounded.

▷ Temporary Setback

Hopes for a continued exchange of POWs were scuttled by South Korean President Rhee in June 1953. Rhee suddenly and unexpectedly released 27,000 North Korean POWs and ordered the South Korean people to shelter them.

Rhee claimed that the United States had betrayed South Korea during the peace talks by not demanding the unification of the two Koreas. His actions temporarily halted the peace talks, but eventually made the two sides even more determined to negotiate a peaceful end to the war.

The peace talks resumed after President Eisenhower sent Assistant Secretary of State Walter Robertson to talk with Rhee. Robertson bluntly told Rhee that reunification was out of the question. In return for Rhee's cooperation, the United States promised a long-term commitment of financial and military aid to South Korea.

With Rhee no longer an obstruction, the truce talks resumed on July 10. Then it only took seventeen days to reach a settlement. The war that was called a police action would be ended by an armistice. An armistice is not a peace treaty, but is more like a truce in which two sides agree to stop fighting.

Chapter 6

The Never-Ending Conflict

At 10:00 A.M. on July 27, 1953, representatives from the UNC and the North Korean government met at Panmunjom, North Korea, to sign the armistice agreement. After 575 meetings over a two-year period, an agreement was finally reached.

▶ Signing the Armistice

General Nam II of the NKPA and General William K. Harrison of the UNC sat across from each other without speaking. After signing nine copies of the agreement in twelve minutes, they quietly left. Neither side could claim victory. There were no handshakes, smiles, or words exchanged. There was only quiet relief that the shooting had finally stopped.

A few hours later, copies of the armistice were also

The armistice between North and South Korea resulted in South Korea's gain of 1,500 square miles, the creation of a buffer zone between the two countries, and the settlement of the POW issue.

signed by UNC General Mark Clark; the Chinese commander, General Peng The-haui; and the North Korean leader, Kim Il Sung.

In his memoirs, General Clark bitterly noted his deep regret at being ". . . the first U.S. Army commander in history to sign an armistice without victory."[1]

▶ Terms of Agreement

The armistice agreement established a demilitarized (no-fire) zone as a buffer between North and South Korea. The zone (also known as the DMZ), was 2.5 miles wide and stretched across the Korean peninsula from the Yellow Sea on the west coast to the Sea of Japan on the east coast.

South Korea gained about 1,500 square miles of territory, but it came at a terrible price. It is estimated that South Korea sustained about one million civilian deaths and that North Korea suffered 2 million civilian deaths. Historians think that a total of 3 to 4 million Korean soldiers and civilians perished in the war. Prior to the war, the combined population of North and South Korea was around 30 million.

The armistice also settled the issue of exchanging POWs. Any POWs who did not want to return to their homeland were placed in the custody of the Neutral Nations Repatriation Committee. A total of 14,227 Chinese, 7,582 North Koreans, 325 South Koreans, 21 Americans, and one British POW refused to return home. Eventually, 137 of the over twenty-two thousand POWs changed their minds.

The armistice provided no permanent peace agreement. Officially, North and South Korea are still at war. Provisions were made for a political conference to work out a final settlement. In 1954, Soviet officials met with

Tools   Search   Notes   Discuss   Go!

Arlington National Cemetery - Microsoft Internet Explorer

File Edit View Favorites Tools Help

Address http://www.americaslibrary.gov/jb/civil/jb_civil_arlington_1_e.html   Go

Arlington National Cemetery

BACK

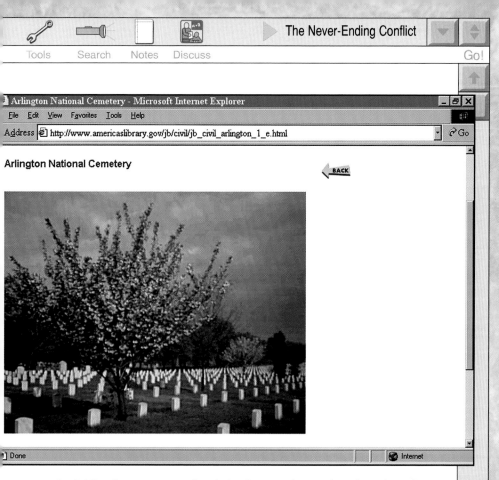

Done   Internet

▲ *Soldiers from every war fought by the United States have been buried in the Arlington National Cemetery. The Tomb of the Unknowns, located on the cemetery's grounds, holds the remains of unidentified servicemen, including those that fought in the Korean War.*

representatives of nations who fought in the Korean War. However, they were unable to draw up a permanent agreement for peace.

▶ Bad Blood

Since the truce, relations between North and South Korea have remained hostile. Shortly after the armistice, both sides accused the other of torturing and starving POWs. Historical records show that both sides were guilty of atrocities such as the execution of civilians and POWs.

There have been repeated incidents along the DMZ since the armistice. It is estimated that over one thousand people were killed in sporadic skirmishes in the first fifty years the DMZ was in place.

In 1971, North and South Korea held reunification talks, but no agreement was reached. When South Korea hosted the 1988 Summer Olympics, North Korea asked to cohost. South Korea refused the request, so North Korea boycotted the event.

Hopes for reunification suffered a further setback in 1991, when North Korea and South Korea joined the United Nations as separate nations.

In the past few years, there have been some serious incidents between North and South Korea. On June 15, 1999, a South Korean vessel sank a North Korean torpedo boat and damaged a second torpedo boat. Between twenty and thirty North Korean sailors were killed.

Three years later, there was a similar incident involving North and South Korean patrol boats in the Yellow Sea. The incident occurred about forty miles off the west coast of the Korean peninsula. Four South Korean sailors were killed and between twenty and thirty were wounded. North Korea acknowledged that it suffered losses, but they did not provide any details. South Korea put its military forces on a state of high alert, but the crisis did not escalate into more fighting.

▷ Renewed Tensions

On January 29, 2002, in his State of the Union address, President George W. Bush called North Korea, Iran, and Iraq nations that formed an "axis of evil." He felt they threatened world peace with weapons of mass destruction.[2] This upset the North Koreans because they felt

▲ *The Korean War Veterans Memorial was erected in 1995 in Washington, D.C., to honor those who fought in what was to be labeled "the forgotten war."*

Bush was saying that the governments of these countries were led by evil people.

In October 2002, North Korea admitted to the United States that it had secretly been working on a nuclear weapons program. The United States sees North Korea as a threat to its allies, especially South Korea and Japan. The hope is that North Korea will give up its nuclear program in exchange for improved trade with the United States. This may help bring relief to the many starving people in North Korea.[3] More communication between the United States, North Korea, and South Korea may help keep the peace, but reuniting the two Korean nations seems less likely.

Chapter Notes

Korean War Facts

1. Casualty figures vary from source to source. These figures are from the 2002 edition of the *World Book Encyclopedia*.

Chapter 1. Predawn Attack

1. David McCullough, *Truman* (New York: Simon & Schuster, 1992), pp. 776–777.

Chapter 2. Korea From 1910 to 1945

1. Clay Blair, *The Forgotten War: America in Korea 1950–1953* (New York: Anchor Books, 1987), p. 81.

2. David McCullough, *Truman* (New York: Simon & Schuster, 1992), p. 782.

3. Ibid.

4. Ibid.

Chapter 3. Early Problems Are Overcome

1. Joseph C. Goulden, *Korea: The Untold Story of the War* (New York: Times Books, 1982), p. 123.

2. Clay Blair, *The Forgotten War: American in Korea 1950–1953* (New York: Anchor Books, 1987), p. 168.

3. Stanley Sandler, *The Korean War: No Victors, No Vanquished* (Lexington: The University Press of Kentucky, 1999), p. 195.

Chapter 4. Back-and-Forth

1. Department of Public Information, "Resolution of 27 June 1950," *Security Council Resolutions: 1950*, n.d., <http://www.un.org/documents/sc/res/1950/scres50.htm> (April 17, 2003).

2. Joseph C. Goulden, *Korea: The Untold Story of the War* (New York: Times Books, 1982), p. 239.

3. Max Hastings, The Korean War (New York: Touchstone Books, 1987), p. 138.

Chapter 5. End of the Fighting

1. David McCullough, *Truman* (New York: Simon & Schuster, 1992), p. 912.

2. Max Hastings, *The Korean War* (New York: Touchstone Books, 1987), p. 317.

3. Stephen E. Ambrose, *Eisenhower: Soldier and President* (New York: Touchstone Books, 1990), p. 285.

Chapter 6. The Never-Ending Conflict

1. Max Hastings, *The Korean War* (New York: Touchstone Books, 1987), p. 325.

2. George W. Bush, "The President's State of the Union Address," *The White House*, January 29, 2002, <http://www.whitehouse.gov/news/releases/2002/01/20020129-11.html> (April 17, 2003).

3. Arshad Mohammed, "U.S. Sees No Swift Breakthrough with N. Korea," *Washington Post.com*, April 16, 2003, <http://www.washingtonpost.com/wp-dyn/articles/A39082-2003Apr16.html> (April 17, 2003).

Further Reading

Alter, Judy. *Harry S Truman*. Berkeley Heights, N.J.: MyReportlinks.com Books, 2002.

Dolan, Jr., Edward F. *America in the Korean War*. Brookfield, Conn.: Millbrook Press, Inc., 1998.

Feinberg, Barbara Silberdick. *Douglas MacArthur: American Hero*. Danbury, Conn.: Franklin Watts, 1999.

Gay, Kathlyn and Martin K. Gay. *The Korean War*. Brookfield, Conn.: Twenty-First Century Books, Incorporated, 1996.

McGowen, Tom. *The Korean War*. Danbury, Conn.: Franklin Watts, 1993.

Rice, Jr., Earle. *The Inchon Invasion: Battles of the Twentieth Century*. Farmington Hills, Mich.: Gale Group, 1996.

Sanford, William R. *Korean War Soldier at Heartbreak Ridge*. Danbury, Conn.: Children's Press, 1991.

Stein, R. Conrad. *The Korean War Veterans Memorial*. Danbury, Conn.: Children's Press, 2002.

———. *The Korean War: "The Forgotten War."* Berkeley Heights, N.J.: Enslow Publishers, Inc., 1994.

Strait, Sandy. *What Was It Like in the Korean War?* Unionville, N.Y.: Royal Fireworks Publishing Company, 1999.

———. *What Really Happened to America's POWs in Korea*. Unionville, N.Y.: Royal Fireworks Publishing Company, 1997.

Index